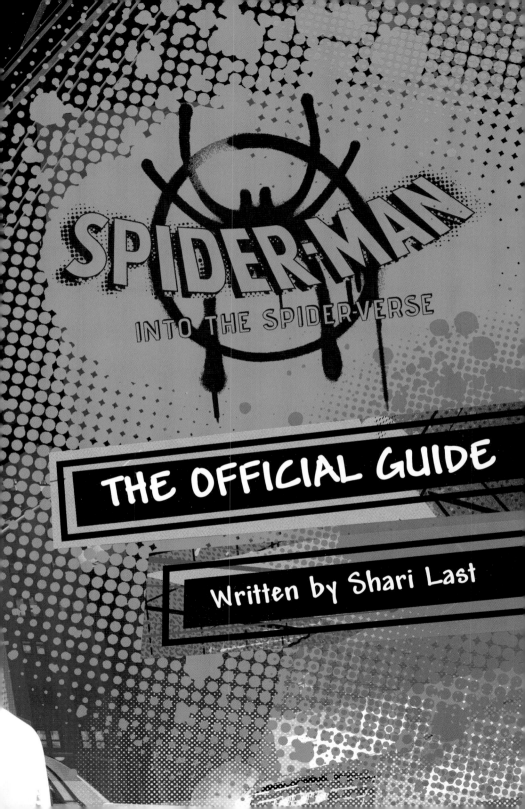

SPIDER-MAN
INTO THE SPIDER-VERSE

THE OFFICIAL GUIDE

Written by Shari Last

CONTENTS

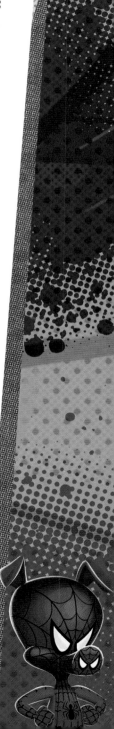

INTRODUCTION

Miles Morales is just a regular kid. He lives in Brooklyn, New York, and is a big fan of the city's favorite Super Hero, Spider-Man. But when Miles gets bitten by a weird-looking spider, it looks like his whole world is about to change...

6

MILES MORALES

Hero in the making

Miles is a smart, friendly kid. He loves making his friends laugh, but he can't seem to focus at school. Learning to be Spider-Man is going to be a real challenge.

Things you need to know about Miles

 1 He loves climbing and jumping his way round the city—a sport called parkour.

 2 He always forgets to tie his shoes.

 3 Miles makes jokes when he's feeling awkward.

 4 He can't wait to learn some awesome Spider-Man moves. If only someone would teach him.

HARD WORK

Miles just started at a new school, Brooklyn Visions Academy. It's a high-tech sleepaway school for Brooklyn's smartest kids. Miles is bright, but there's so much to learn! He sometimes worries that he can't handle it.

Odd one out

Miles often feels like he doesn't completely fit in at school. Everyone else seems like they've got things under control.

SPIDER BITE

Miles and his uncle Aaron are spray-painting in an abandoned subway tunnel. But Miles is unaware of something creeping and crawling its way down toward him.

Bag full of Uncle Aaron's spray paints

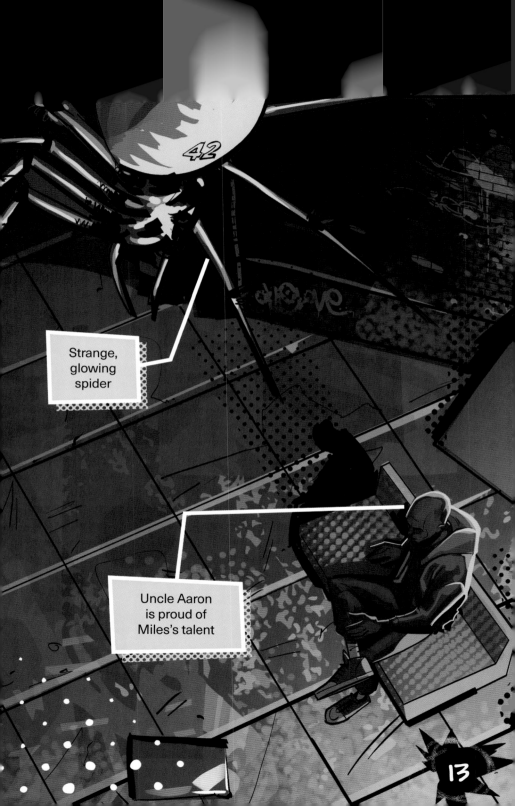

Invisibility

Wall-crawling

Stickiness

Enhanced agility

Spider-sense

NEW POWERS

Miles has grown overnight, has a new, tingly spider-sense, and is suddenly very, very sticky. There's only one possible explanation: he's becoming Spider-Man! Miles can't wait to test out his new super powers.

STICKING OUT

Although he tries to fit in at school, Miles can't help causing a scene when his new-found stickiness gets out of control! Miles is hopeful that his classmates might not have noticed...

1 It's Wanda, a new girl from Miles's physics class.

2 Miles tries to be friendly, but his hand gets stuck!

3 Wanda is not impressed. Look at her hair! Oops.

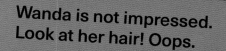

4 Looks like it'll be some time before Wanda forgives him.

GANKE

Man of few words

Ganke is Miles's roommate at school. Not that Miles knows his name—Ganke is so obsessed with his comic books, computer, and music, he hasn't actually introduced himself to Miles yet.

Things you need to know about Ganke

1. He is a Spider-Man and comics superfan.

2. His computer is his LIFE.

3. Ganke has a truly impressive collection of comic books.

4. He is actually pretty cool, once you get to know him.

Did you know?
One of Ganke's all-time favorite comics is *The Amazing Spider-Man*.

SUPERFAN

Ganke is a huge comic book fan. He loves his comics so much that he's hardly looked at his new roommate Miles, let alone talked to him! Ganke knows almost everything about Spider-Man. ALMOST.

In his own world

If only Ganke would look up for a second, he might see a real-life Spider-Man in front of his very eyes!

TOP TEACHERS

Miles likes learning new things, even if Brooklyn Visions is a little homework heavy. He has lots of great teachers. If only he could focus long enough in class!

SOME OF MILES'S CLASSES

Advanced Physics
Cool theories, but tricky math.

Chemistry
Awesome experiments!

American History
Important to know, but a lot to learn!

Trigonometry
Sounds smart,
but very confusing.

Literature
Great stories—but
lots of reading.

Computer Science
Super useful but SO.
MANY. SYMBOLS.

"Just because it's hard,
doesn't mean you can't
rise to the challenge."
Miles's dad, Jefferson

JEFFERSON DAVIS

Old-school Brooklyn cop

Miles's dad, Jefferson, wants to keep the city safe. He is proud that his son Miles goes to a top school. If only Miles would try his best. And tie his shoes.

Things you need to know about Jefferson

1 He prides himself on being a good, honest cop.

2 Jefferson will never run a red light—unless on official duty.

3 He thinks catching bad guys is a job for the police only.

4 Jefferson finds Spider-Man a *teeny*, tiny bit annoying.

Did you know?

Jefferson is known for being one of the most honest police officers in the force.

26

Need a ride?
It's kind of embarrassing being driven to school in a police car, but that's what happens when your dad is a cop!

FATHER AND SON

Lately, Jefferson finds it hard to connect with Miles. Maybe it's just a teenager thing, but Jefferson wishes his son would open up to him a little more.

RIO MORALES

Amazing mom

Miles's mom, Rio, is warm and caring. She loves Miles more than anything. Rio knows that life can be confusing and overwhelming. She hopes Miles will confide in her when he needs to.

Things you need to know about Rio

1 She is one of the most popular nurses at the local hospital.

2 Rio is from Puerto Rico and speaks fluent Spanish.

3 She doesn't mind embarrassing Miles by kissing him in public!

4 Rio believes that everything feels better in the morning.

RIGHT AT HOME

When he's not at school, Miles lives with his parents. His bedroom might be a mess, but he knows where everything is, from his headphones to his sketchpad. (Hint: they're usually on the floor!)

Downtown Brooklyn

Miles loves his friendly neighbors. When he walks out of his front door, he knows almost everyone, and he enjoys catching up.

Did you know?
Miles wants to tell his mom and dad about his new powers, but he also wants to keep his new hero identity secret.

LOVING PARENTS

Rio and Jefferson love Miles very much. They work hard at their jobs and try to be good role models for their son. They are proud of the kind, honest, and strong-minded kid he has become.

Phone a friend

Miles loves his parents too, but sometimes it's just easier to confide in his uncle, Aaron.

AARON DAVIS

Carefree uncle

Cool, fun, and a little bit reckless, Uncle Aaron coudn't be more different to his brother, Jefferson. No one really knows what Aaron's day job is, but he enjoys a close bond with his nephew Miles.

Things you need to know about Aaron

1 He used to sneak Miles chocolate, when Miles was a kid.

2 Aaron is an amazing graffiti artist.

3 Somehow, he knows all the coolest secret spots in the city.

4 Aaron and Jefferson don't really get along so well.

Up and over

Aaron and Miles hop a tall fence to access an abandoned subway tunnel, far below the city.

RULE BREAKER

Uncle Aaron isn't afraid to break the rules. He thinks rules are boring. So when Miles sneaks out of school, Aaron is happy to take him on a nighttime adventure.

"You're an artist, Miles.
Do it your own way."
Uncle Aaron

Fire escape is a handy access route for Miles

AARON'S APARTMENT

Miles sometimes feels a little out of place at his fancy school. Luckily, he has somewhere to escape to when the pressure gets too much. Uncle Aaron always welcomes Miles to his apartment.

SPIDER-MAN

New York's famous hero

It's the amazing, web-slinging, wall-climbing, suit-wearing Spider-Man! The one and only! Oh, wait—this guy is not the only Spider-Man any more...

Things you need to know about Spider-Man

1 He has saved New York countless times.

2 His archenemy is the Green Goblin.

3 He was also bitten by a radioactive spider many years ago.

4 Spider-Man has no clue that there are other Spider-People out there

SPIDEY SUIT

Miles knows all about Spider-Man.
He's seen him on TV and his roommate
Ganke has all the comic books. If Miles
wants to become Spider-Man, the first
thing he needs is the suit.

Shopping trip

OK, so buying a Spider-Man costume isn't quite the same as thinking up your own suit. Still, it's good enough for now, right?

PETER PARKER

Unexpected ally

Peter Parker is Spider-Man—but he comes from a parallel universe! He promises to teach Miles to be Spider-Man. Miles has a feeling he won't be a very good teacher...

Things you need to know about Peter

 1 He has been his world's only Spider-Man for 16 years.

 2 He is not a fan of capes.

 3 At first, Peter doesn't want to help Miles, but later changes his mind.

 4 He can even walk down the sides of buildings, while standing vertically.

Did you know?
Peter promises to teach Miles how to be Spider-Man, but he doesn't mean it!

Hero or zero?

Peter doesn't look how Miles thought a Super Hero would look. He hasn't shaved in a while—and by the way he devours a burger, he probably hasn't eaten in a while, either!

TIRED HERO

Peter Parker has been Spider-Man for a long time. A very long time. He's saved the world again and again —and he's a little fed up with all the bad guys, all the hard work, and all the responsibility.

SPIDEY SAYS

Peter Parker knows what it takes to be Spider-Man. He gives Miles plenty of advice. But is Peter's expert advice good or bad? That's for Miles to decide…

1 "Take my advice and ignore your powers."

2 "You can't think about saving the world. You have to think about saving one person."

3 "Don't watch the mouth. Watch the hands."

4 "You need a mask."

5 "Baby powder in the suit. Heavy on the joints."

6 "I'm in charge."

7 "Don't do it like me. Do it like you."

51

SPIDER-GWEN

Team leader

Spider-Gwen is smart and fearless. She is full of ideas and never wastes time worrying about things she can't control. When Gwen uses her Spider powers, she is almost unstoppable.

Things you need to know about Spider-Gwen

 Spider-Gwen's real name is Gwen Stacy.

 She is a Super Hero from a different universe.

 She has been Spider-Gwen for two years.

 Gwen does NOT appreciate it when people call her "doll."

52

LEADER

Spider-Gwen might be in a new universe, but that doesn't stop her from building a team of Super Heroes and coming up with a plan to help everyone get back to where they belong.

Listen up

When Gwen speaks, people listen. She is smart and strong-willed, but also friendly and kind. Her teammates are happy to follow her.

Did you know?

Gwen's spider-sense told her to go to Miles's school. She pretended her name was Wanda.

SPIDER-HAM

No joke

Spider-Ham is a cartoon pig, but no one takes their job as a Super Hero more seriously. He is funny and deeply loyal, as well as being a master of his Spider powers.

Things you need to know about Spider-Ham

 1 His real name is Peter Porker.

 2 He comes from a parallel Earth, known as Earth–8311.

3 He likes to make "oink" noises and pretend he can't speak when meeting people.

 4 Spider-Ham fights in a cartoon cloud of fury!

SPIDER-MAN NOIR

Hero from the past

Spider-Man Noir finds modern New York confusing—it's nothing like the city he protects in his world. Still, a villain's a villain, and Noir knows all about catching them!

Things you need to know about Spider-Man Noir

 1 Noir is from Earth–90214, an Earth in a parallel universe.

 2 Spider-Man Noir's world is all black and white.

 3 He gets pretty cranky when people sneak up on him.

 4 He doesn't really get jokes.

PENI PARKER

Tech-savvy Spidey

Young, strong-willed Peni Parker is from a future version of New York. She controls a powerful Spider-Man robot known as SP//dr. Together, they have Spider powers.

Things you need to know about Peni

1 Her special skill is making SP//dr do the robot dance. It's a real crowd pleaser.

2 Peni is a coding expert.

3 She loves having a giggle, but she can be quite feisty, too!

4 She is from Earth–14512 in a parallel universe.

Under control

SP//dr was designed by Peni Parker's father and it responds only to her DNA. Peni can ride inside SP//dr or control it from afar.

SP//dr

Peni Parker's robot, SP//dr, is one of a kind. Its red-and-blue metal body is strong, flexible, and fast. It can punch through walls, chase down villains, and curl into a ball to avoid detection.

SPIDER-VERSE

Miles is shocked to discover that his new Spider friends are all from different universes. Somehow, they have been transported to Miles's world by a mysterious machine that has been built under the city. Incredible!

Spider-Man
Peter Parker comes from a world that is almost the same as Miles's world.

Spider-Man Noir
The black and white streets of New York past are kept safe by Spider-Man Noir.

Peni Parker

The people in future New York have never heard of Peter Parker. Peni is their hero.

Spider-Ham

Cartoon pig heroes are completely normal in Spider-Ham's world.

Spider-Gwen

Back in Gwen's world, she has a friend called Peter Parker. He's just a regular kid.

65

AUNT MAY

Trusted ally

Peter Parker's aunt, May, has the sweetest little old lady face, but don't be fooled. May is no helpless bystander—she gives the Spider team a place to call home and plenty of good advice.

Things you need to know about May

 1 May lives in a small terraced house in Queens.

 2 Her garden shed looks ordinary... but it isn't.

3 It is May who gives Miles his Spidey suit.

 4 She can hold her own in a fight!

WHICH SPIDER HERO ARE YOU?

There are so many different Spider Super Heroes. Take the quiz to find out what sort of hero you would be!

1 How would you describe your personality?

A   Positive
B   Serious
C   Cheerful

2 How would you train a new Super Hero?

A   Lots of helpful advice
B   Practice, practice, practice
C   Encourage them to keep trying

3 What's your favorite color?

A   Turquoise
B   Black
C   Red and blue!

4 What is your best quality?

A Confidence
B Determination
C Sense of humor

5 You've forgotten your web-shooters. Do you:

A Take a huge leap. You know you can do it.
B Think hard. Can you build a bridge if you work really fast?
C Call your friends. They'll help you out.

Mostly As
Spider-Gwen

You are fearless. You are a born leader and people listen to you because you are so positive.

Mostly Bs
Spider-Man Noir

You are hard-working and focused. You will not stop until you've completed your task.

Mostly Cs
Spider-Ham

You are friendly and encouraging. You get the best out of people by being kind.

GREEN GOBLIN

Mean, green fighting machine

Big, green, and terrifying, the Green Goblin is Spider-Man's archenemy. This Super Villain is unnaturally strong, fierce in battle, and scary to look at!

Things you need to know about Green Goblin

1 When he's not being a monster, his real name is Norman Osborn.

2 He is 22 feet (6.7 meters) tall—as tall as a two-story building!

3 The Green Goblin can fly, thanks to a pair of wings on his back.

4 His tongue is huge—and BLUE!

KINGPIN

In the business of crime

Kingpin is the big boss. And he's really, really big. This hulking man is famous for being a ruthless businessman. Less commonly known is that he is also the leader of New York's criminal underworld.

Things you need to know about Kingpin

1. Real name Wilson Fisk.

2. Kingpin is in control of everything that goes on in the city. (Or so he thinks.)

3. He only wears the best suits that money can buy.

4. Kingpin does not like failure.

Unexpected results

Kingpin's super collider is a huge machine. It uses lots of energy to carry out never-before-seen experiments. Kinpgin has no idea how powerful it really is.

SECRET PLAN

Kingpin is always up to something. Right now, his top-secret plan is the construction of a super collider. He is excited about what it can do, but he hasn't thought about the dangers.

Did you know?
A super collider fires particles at top speeds to see what happens when they collide.

PROWLER

City stalker

Always on the hunt, Prowler is a dangerous foe. He is a stealthy villain, with an exceptional knowledge of the city. He has no super powers, but he makes up for that with his weapons-packed Prowler suit.

Things you need to know about Prowler

 1 The razor sharp claws on his gloves can slice through a table.

 2 His true identity is a closely guarded secret.

 3 His rocket boots enable him to fly for short distances.

 4 His helmet has infra-red vision.

High-speed chase

Prowler and a motorbike make for a deadly combination.
He can zip easily through the city's streets, chasing his prey.

ON THE HUNT

Prowler is known and feared for the skill with which he stalks his enemies. He uses infra-red vision to track his prey in the dark, while his suit blends in to the shadows.

Did you know?
Kingpin hired Prowler for his expert stalking abilities.

TOMBSTONE

Not to be messed with

Tombstone is one of Kingpin's fierce and deadly henchmen. He is scarily tall and strong. Tombstone's greatest skill is being able to intimidate most of his foes without uttering even a single word.

Things you need to know about Tombstone

1. Real name Lonnie Lincoln.

2. His grayish skin makes people think he is a ghost or a zombie.

3. His mouth is full of sharp, spiky teeth that he filed himself.

4. As a kid, he was bullied at school.

SCORPION

Poisonous beast

Half man, half gigantic insect, Scorpion makes everyone run for cover. His greatest super power is his strength. His tail is powerful enough to crush an enemy.

Things you need to know about Scorpion

1 He has one human arm and one scorpion pincer.

2 His tail shoots toxic acid.

3 Scorpion can climb walls and hang from ceilings thanks to his four mechanical legs.

4 He is one angry guy!

TOP TIPS

Becoming Spider-Man is not as simple as just being bitten by a spider. That's the easy part. It takes courage, patience, and perseverance to become a Super Hero. And, of course, making a LOT of mistakes.

MILES'S TOP TIPS FOR BUDDING SUPER HEROES

1

Don't panic.
Super powers are CRAZY! But you can do it. You got this.

2 **Take your time.**
Yes, it's scary. Only
leap when you're ready.

3 **Don't look down.**
Seriously, don't do it.

"No matter how many hits I take, I always find a way to come back."

Miles

AWESOME MOVES

It took a while, and lots of practice, but Miles has finally mastered his Spidey powers. He is a true Spider-Man.

Venom Strike

Just one touch and BOOM! Enemy is blasted away.

The Upside Downer

Dive down, then shoot a web upward to stick to a building.

Double Flip
Makes escaping from an enemy's grasp a piece of cake.

Swing 'n' Save
Leap in, save the hostage, leap out. Simple.

WHAT'S YOUR SPIDER POWER?

Miles has gained lots of amazing super powers, including some that other Spider heroes don't seem to have! Which super Spider power would you have?

Start

Do you love running, jumping, and being really active?

Yes

Are you scared of heights?

Yes

No

No

Can you think fast under pressure?

No

Can you be stealthy?

No

Yes

94

INCREASED BALANCE

INVISIBILITY

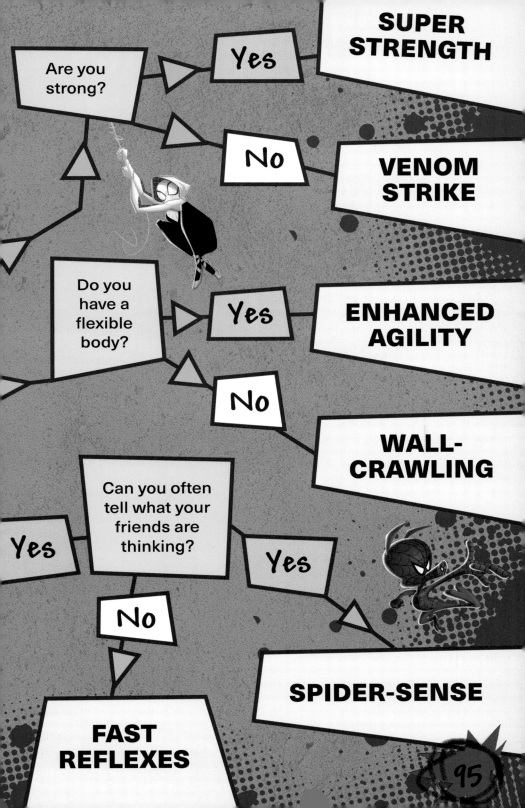

SUPER STRENGTH

Are you strong?

Yes

No

VENOM STRIKE

Do you have a flexible body?

Yes

ENHANCED AGILITY

No

WALL-CRAWLING

Can you often tell what your friends are thinking?

Yes

Yes

No

SPIDER-SENSE

FAST REFLEXES

Penguin
Random
House

Written and edited by Shari Last
Senior Designer Lynne Moulding
Senior Pre-Production Producer Jennifer Murray
Senior Producer Mary Slater
Managing Editor Sadie Smith
Managing Art Editor Vicky Short
Publisher Julie Ferris
Art Director Lisa Lanzarini
Publishing Director Simon Beecroft

First American Edition, 2018
Published in the United States by DK Publishing
345 Hudson Street, New York, New York 10014

DK, a Division of Penguin Random House LLC
18 19 20 21 10 9 8 7 6 5 4 3 2 1
001–310699–Nov/2018

Published in Great Britain by Dorling Kindersley Limited.

A catalog record for this book is available
from the Library of Congress.

ISBN: 978-1-4654-7746-0

DK books are available at special discounts when
purchased in bulk for sales promotions, premiums,
fund-raising, or educational use.
For details, contact: DK Publishing Special Markets,
345 Hudson Street, New York, New York 10014
SpecialSales@dk.com

Printed and bound in the USA

A WORLD OF IDEAS:
SEE ALL THERE IS TO KNOW

www.dk.com
www.marvel.com